PROJECTS FOR SPRING

& HOLIDAY ACTIVITIES

Celia McInnes

Illustrated by Malcolm Walker

WITHDRAWN

C.1

Seasonal Projects
Projects for Spring & Holiday Activities
Projects for Summer & Holiday Activities
Projects for Autumn & Holiday Activities
Projects for Winter & Holiday Activities
Projects for Christmas & Holiday Activities
Projects for Easter & Holiday Activities

Seasons do not happen at the same time of year everywhere. In the northern and southern halves of the world the seasons are reversed, as this chart shows:

Northern Hemisphere			
Spring	*Summer*	*Autumn*	*Winter*
March	June	September	December
April	July	October	January
May	August	November	February
Autumn	*Winter*	*Spring*	*Summer*
Southern Hemisphere			

©1989 by Garrett Educational Corporation
First published in the United States in 1989 by
Garrett Educational Corporation, 130 East 13th Street,
Ada, OK 74820

First published in 1988 by Wayland (Publishers) Limited,
England
©1988 Wayland (Publishers) Limited, England

Typeset in England
Printed in Italy
Bound in USA

Library of Congress Cataloging-in-Publication Data

McInnes, Celia
    Projects for spring & holiday activities.

    (Seasonal projects)
    Includes index.
    Summary: Presents arts and crafts projects, recipes, games, and activities associated with the Spring season.
    1. Creative activities and seat work—Juvenile literature. 2. Spring—Juvenile literature. [1. Handicraft. 2. Spring] I. Walker, Malcolm, ill. II. Title. III. Series.
GV1203.M356   1989   649.5   88-33514
ISBN 0-944483-40-2

Cover/top left *Making a torn-paper collage of a Beltane bonfire.*

Cover/top right *A watercress hedgehog.*

Cover/bottom *Children taking part in the May Day custom of dancing around the maypole.*

Contents

THE COUNTRYSIDE IN SPRING

As the weather improves in the spring we look forward to getting out into the countryside. Make your outing more interesting by looking out for things.

Why not keep your eyes open for materials that could, on your return, be made into a countryside collage.

While you enjoy yourself, picking flowers and fruits and going for walks, remember the countryside is also a place where people make a living. So always follow the Country Code:

● Do not drop litter or light fires. Farm animals or wild creatures could be hurt, and the land spoiled.
● You should not pick flowers unless there are a lot of that particular sort around. Do not pick a plant you think could be a rare species.
● Do not trample the crops.

In spring there are lots of young animals out in the fields. You need to be very careful not to disturb them.

● Do not leave gates open because animals might escape.

● Never dig up wild plants.
● Never catch wild birds or animals.

COUNTRYSIDE COLLAGE

Look for:
● Common wild flowers such as clover, dandelions, buttercups, violets and daisies. Notice which flowers grow in different places, such as in fields or marshlands.
● Useful greenery, such as oak and ash leaves. Look at the difference in their shapes. Notice how prickly holly, soft fern leaves and sticky yard grass all feel very different.
● Plant seeds, grains and grasses.
● Fallen pine needles, strips of birch bark, feathers and some soft pussy willow or cattails.

You will need:
- stiff cardboard
- glue
- a pair of scissors
- sheets of blotting paper
- a heavy book
- the natural materials you have collected

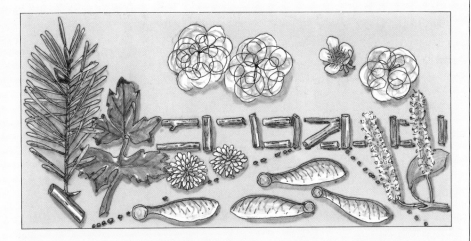

1 Create your own countryside by gluing items from your collection onto the card. Make a pussy willow bud into a field mouse, fern leaves into tiny trees, a plant into a bush and so on.

2 Press some of the flowers and leaves flat before you glue them to the card. To do this, put them between sheets of blotting paper and place a heavy book on top.

3 You can also use ivy and oak leaves to make skeletons for your collage. Put the leaves in rainwater until all the soft green "flesh" rots away. Only their fine network of veins is left.

MAKE A SEASIDE COLLAGE

If you go to the seaside at this time, collect items for a sea-world collage. Look out for the various types of seaweed, which look and feel very different. Pick up tiny stones and shells, worn-away pieces of driftwood, gulls' feathers and perhaps even the remains of creatures, like crabs' claws or dried starfish. Don't forget to collect some sand, or lots of small pebbles of different shapes and colors, in a plastic bag.

PURIM

To celebrate Purim, adults and children put on fancy clothes and dance to music in the streets. Some of the costumes have little to do with the original story, but this doesn't seem to matter.

Purim is a festival held in February or March. It is a time when Jews remember the story of how Esther saved the lives of all the Jews in Persia (now Iran). Around 500 BC King Ahazuerus of Persia had a minister called Haman who hated all Jews because one, called Mordecai, would not bow down to him but would honor only God. So Haman persuaded the king to have all Jews put to death. Hearing of this, Queen Esther invited Haman to a banquet at the palace then told the king why Haman wanted to destroy the Jews. She said that she too would have to die because she was Jewish, something the king had not known. Ahazuerus, angry at being tricked by Haman, executed him instead and appointed Mordecai in his place.

At Purim, the story of Esther is read aloud or acted as a play. Whenever Haman's name is mentioned everyone makes as much noise as possible, booing, stamping and using noisemakers known as "greggars." In some places Purim has become a time of carnival. Parades with big models of Haman go through the streets. Sometimes these models are burned on a bonfire. People also eat a special three-cornered biscuit called Hamantashen, which is supposed to symbolize Haman's hat, his pocket or his ear!

GLOVE PUPPETS

Act out the Purim story using simple felt glove puppets. Make Haman look really menacing, with fierce eyes, bold eyebrows and perhaps a little beard.

Give Esther and Ahazuerus stitched-on crowns and Mordecai a wooden staff. This can be held in place by gluing velcro to the staff and his hand.

For each puppet you will need:
- **two pieces of felt, each about 11 × 9 in.**
- **felt scraps for features**
- **wool or string**
- **pins, needle and thread**
- **fabric glue**

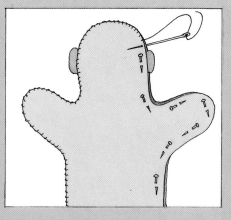

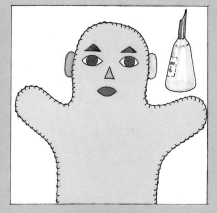

1 Cut the felt pieces into a shape like a mitten with a thumb on each side. Pin the pieces together. If you like, insert ears between the two layers of felt and pin them in place. You could also pin a hat or headdress on the outside of the main pieces.

2 Sew around with tiny stitches, except along the bottom where your hand goes in.

3 Glue on cut-out felt eyes, mouth and nose. If you like, oversew with thread to make sure they do not fall off; or use buttons or beads, sewn in place.

4 For the eyebrows, moustache, beard and hair, add felt pieces, or sew on wool or frayed string instead.

MOTHER'S DAY

On the fourth Sunday in Lent, the Christian Church used to require everyone to visit the main church in the district, known as the "mother church." It was a happy day of reunions. Also on that day the Lenten fast was relaxed.

The day became known as Mothering Sunday and referred to the mother of the family as well as the mother church. It was often the only time of the year when children working away from home as servants were allowed to visit their family. The custom of taking mother little presents of flowers and cakes developed. Simnel cake was popular, made with a flour called "simila."

Mother's Day is an American idea that has become connected in Europe with the old Mothering Sunday. It was started by an American, Anna Jarvis, early this century and is officially held in the United States on the second Sunday in May.

On Mother's Day we remember our mother. We say thank you for all she does for us throughout the year by giving her little presents and flowers, and perhaps even helping her around the house.

AN OLD-FASHIONED SAMPLER

Make your mother an alphabet sampler for Mother's Day. It should include the numbers 1-10, the letters of the alphabet, your name and the date, and some decorations, such as simple flowers and different colored lines. If you like, include a short rhyme, such as "North South East West, Home Is Best."

You will need:
- **canvas (6 holes to each 1 in. is a good size)**
- **embroidery silks or wool**
- **a blunt-ended tapestry needle**
- **graph paper**

First, work out the spacing on a piece of paper. Try to use graph paper with the same number of squares to the inch as the canvas has holes to the inch.

1 Copy your design onto the canvas in pencil, drawing from hole to hole.

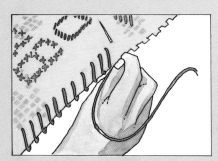

2 Stitch over the pencil lines using a back stitch or cross stitch.

3 Finish by oversewing the outside edges to prevent fraying.

AN EASY MOTHER'S DAY CARD

You will need:
- stiff paper
- a pair of scissors
- crayons or colored pens

1 Fold a rectangle of paper lengthwise and cut into the folded edge about a quarter of the way down the fold.

2 Unfold the paper and refold it in half the opposite way. Fold again so the cut is inside the card.

3 Pull the cut outward and crease along the dotted lines shown above. The "beak" opens and closes with the card.

4 Draw a bird around the beak and write your greeting inside it.

5 Decorate the rest of the card with things your mother likes.

HOLI OR HOLA MOHALLA

Holi is celebrated by Hindus everywhere and is especially important in northern India. It usually falls in March. It is a joyful festival to give thanks for the spring wheat harvest. People light bonfires and may roast and eat offerings of the winter barley. They sometimes smear the ashes on their foreheads to bring good luck in the coming year.

The bonfires stand for the triumph of good over evil and household rubbish may be burned as a sign that any past wrongs are forgiven. People try to settle their quarrels, pay debts and show goodwill to friends and neighbors. Much visiting and feasting goes on, gifts of candies are exchanged, and nuts and fruit are taken to the temple.

It is a time for fun and games. One widespread custom of Holi is the throwing of colored powders or waters over friends and passers-by for good luck.

There are many different legends about Holi. One concerns the character Holika, and her effigy may sometimes be burned on the bonfire. Another links the festival with the love of the gods Krishna and Radha who are said to have begun the custom of the colored powders.

Throwing colored powder over friends is one of the ways of celebrating the festival of Holi.

The Sikh version of Holi is called Hola Mohalla, and it was begun in 1680 by the Guru Gobind Singh. He organized events such as military exercises, sports, and music and poetry competitions. This tradition has continued. Although there is a certain amount of foolery, on the whole it is a more serious festival. It usually ends with a visit to the gurdwara (temple) to pray for good health.

COCONUT CANDY

Among the special foods eaten at Holi is roasted coconut. This is the Hindu symbol of fruitfulness and new life. Candies are also popular, so combine the customs and make coconut candy. You will need to ask an adult to help you.

You will need:
- **1 lb of sugar**
- **½ cup of milk**
- **½ lb of dried coconut**
- **pink food coloring (if you like)**

1 Bring the sugar and milk slowly to a boil in a heavy saucepan and boil for 3-4 minutes, stirring all the time to dissolve the sugar. Be very careful not to burn yourself.

2 Remove from the heat and add the coconut, still stirring.

3 Pour half the mixture into a well-greased baking tin about ¾-1 in. deep. When it has cooled a little, color the rest and pour on top.

4 When it is firm, mark squares on the surface. When it has set completely, cut it into chunks.

BE A NATURE DETECTIVE

Once life has really started again in spring, become a nature detective and look for signs of wildlife in your area. Make notes and sketches in a nature diary and look them up in reference books when you get home.

To start with you might go around the backyard or local park in search of spiders' webs. Look for the common garden spider's circular "orb" web.

Look for food remains, droppings or tracks that show that a certain animal lives nearby or has passed by. The way food has been eaten is a useful clue. The type of hole made in a nutshell might tell you which animal or bird ate the nuts.

It is possible to tell which animal or bird droppings belong to by looking at their size, color and content. Notice how the droppings made by owls and other predatory birds contain the prey's fur or bones. Where they are found is important too.

Trees may be home to a variety of creatures, from birds like the robin and the woodpecker to the squirrel in its circular nest high up in the branches.

Above left *Freshly dug pile of dirt outside the entrance to a badger's burrow.*
Above right *Squirrels sometimes build their houses inside hollow trees, but often they build them in the branches of trees, using twigs and dried leaves.*

You may find a field mouse's home and a bird's nest at ground level.

Burrows can be seen from open meadowland to edges of highways. It can be difficult to decide which animal lives there. Look carefully for clues, such as food scraps and droppings. Sometimes the smell may help! Stray hairs caught in hedges and on barbed wire are a useful guide.

Watch out for the marks animals leave on their surroundings; for instance, rabbits and deer tear the bark off trees.

If you keep looking and keep quiet you should have a good chance of seeing the creatures themselves and not just the clues!

MAKING A PLASTER CAST OF A TRACK

Keep a record of any animal tracks (or birds' footprints) you find by making a plaster cast of them. Tracks made in soft earth or mud are best for doing this.

You will need:
- **plaster of Paris and water**
- **a strip of cardboard 1 in. deep or a wooden frame**
- **a paperclip**
- **paint**

(Not to scale)

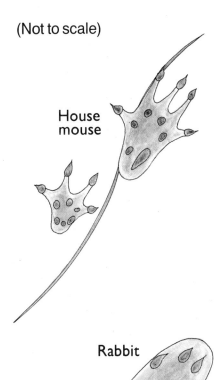

House mouse

Rabbit

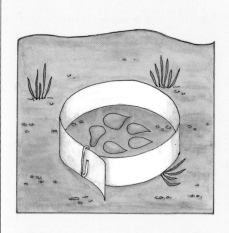

1 Bend the cardboard into a circle large enough to surround the print and secure it with a paperclip. Place over the print.

2 Mix the plaster with water so that it becomes creamy.

3 Pour the plaster mixture into the frame and then leave the cast to harden, probably for 15-30 minutes.

4 Remove the frame. Pick up the plaster and brush off any dirt. Paint the print so that it shows up well. Label it with your name and where and when you found it.

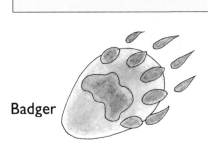

Badger

Squirrel

ST. PATRICK'S DAY

St. Patrick, the patron saint of Ireland, was born in Britain in about AD 385 and was abducted by a band of Irish raiders when he was sixteen. They took him to Ireland where he worked in slavery for six years. During this time he became a deeply religious man.

One day, in a dream, he learned that he was to make his escape from Ireland in a ship. He fled from his captors and eventually reached Britain. But his journey was not easy and he nearly starved to death on the way.

Shortly after his return home, he was called in a dream to return to Ireland to spread the gospel of Christ. So, despite his doubts, he returned to Ireland and preached far and wide.

St. Patrick's emblems are snakes and the shamrock, both of which come from ancient legends about him. He is said to have freed Ireland of its snakes by driving them all into the sea; and when explaining to an unbeliever about the Holy Trinity — three persons in one God — he picked a shamrock and showed him the three leaves on the single stalk.

St. Patrick's feast day is March 17. On this day Irish people wear green and pin shamrocks to their lapels.

Two small boys in San Francisco, California, watch the St. Patrick's Day parade pass by.

PUT ON A PLAY

St. Patrick's life was full of exciting events. You can have fun acting out your own version of his life story.

1 Choose your character. There are Irish raiders, St. Patrick and his family, and the people he preached to. Add any others you like.

2 Decide on your plot. You could begin with the Irish raiders taking St. Patrick away from his family. Make plenty of snakes so that you can act a scene with St. Patrick chasing them into the sea.

3 Make up your own words. You may like to have pairs of rhyming lines and to include lines about the audience.

4 Keep the costumes and makeup simple. The raiders should look very wicked and St. Patrick only needs to have a cloak and a cross.

Make the snakes in lots of different colors and pull them from one side of the stage to the other.

5 Involve the audience as much as possible. You may like to stop briefly and serve the audience a green drink. Make it from lime juice or apple juice, and add green fruit to it, such as grapes, kiwi fruit or chopped apples.

SNAKES

You will need:
- **a grown-up's old pair of colored tights**
- **stuffing, such as rags, tights or chipped foam**
- **scraps of felt**
- **a needle and thread**
- **glue**

1 Cut a leg off the tights, stuff it, and then tie up the open end with some thread.

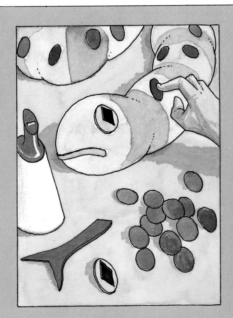

2 Glue felt eyes, a mouth and a long, bright red tongue onto one end. Then glue felt spots of different colors all over the snake's body.

3 Attach a long piece of strong thread or string to the snake's nose and tail so that it can be pulled backward and forward across the floor.

PASSOVER

Passover (Pesach in Hebrew) is the Jewish festival that celebrates the escape of the Israelites from slavery in Egypt many centuries ago. It reminds every Jew of the importance of freedom.

Moses was an Israelite born in Egypt who had fled from the country after killing an Egyptian in a fight. One day he saw a bush that appeared to be burning. At the same time he heard the voice of God telling him to lead his people out of Egypt to a land "flowing with milk and honey." The Pharaoh would not release the Jews, so God sent ten plagues to Egypt. The last of these was the killing of the first-born son in every family. God told the Israelites to mark their own homes with the blood of a lamb so that the Angel of Death would "pass over" them without taking lives. This gives the festival its name.

After this, the Pharaoh let the Israelites go and they made their way across the Red Sea to the Promised Land. The festival is celebrated by a

A traditional family Passover meal.

special meal at which traditional foods are eaten. Unleavened bread (without yeast) is a reminder that the Jews had to leave Egypt so quickly they could not wait for their bread to rise.

CHAROSET

Make some charoset for a Passover meal. Charoset symbolizes the "bricks and mortar" used in building work carried out by the enslaved Israelites. It is a delicious recipe.

You will need:
- **a few eating apples**
- **chopped nuts, raisins and dates**
- **grape juice**
- **cinnamon**

1 Peel and core the apples and chop them finely.

2 Add to them about half as much of the nut and fruit mixture.

3 Flavor with a little cinnamon.

4 Mix to a paste with a little grape juice.

WATERCRESS HEDGEHOG

Passover is, in part, a celebration of spring's return. Why not grow your own spring crop?

You will need:
- **an egg**
- **scraps of damp newspaper or blotting paper**
- **watercress seeds**
- **modeling clay and paint**

1 Hardboil the egg and slice off a piece along the side.

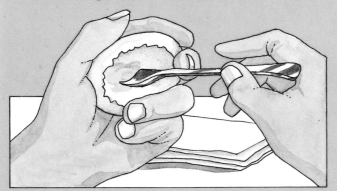

2 Scoop out the inside of the egg and line the shell with damp newspaper or blotting paper.

3 Sprinkle on the watercress seeds and leave them to germinate.

4 In a few days you should have a crop of fresh watercress to eat.

5 To turn your egg into a hedgehog, paint on a face and bristles. Stick on modeling clay for stubby feet and a nose.

APRIL FOOL'S DAY

No one really knows how April Fool's Day (or All Fools' Day) began. It may have been a celebration of the spring equinox — when the day and night are the same length. Or it may have marked the beginning of the old New Year when this fell at the end of March. The Hindu festival of Holi, which is also marked by mischievous foolery, falls at about this time.

The day has been remembered for at least 400 years in France, where children try to pin a "poisson d'Avril" (April fish) onto someone's back.

April 1 is the occasion for playing practical jokes, such as sending children on fruitless errands for "a jar of elbow grease" or "a pound of rubber nails."

Another trick is to ask a schoolfriend to hold one end of a piece of string while you "measure the wall." Go around the corner and ask another friend to hold the other end. Then disappear! Telling someone "your shoelace is undone" never seems to fail. When they look down, call out "April Fool!"

All jokes must happen before night or the joker is the fool, hence:

> April Fool's has already past,
> And you're the biggest fool at last.

Today, television, radio and newspaper items sometimes make April Fools of us. So look out on April 1 or you may be the April Fool.

MAKE A MAGIC WALLET
Trick your friends with this clever wallet.

THIS IS HOW YOU PLAY THE TRICK.

Bet a friend that you can make a dollar bill inserted under the parallel bars of your wallet move under the X by magic.

Close the wallet and turn it around so that you can open it the other way. Say the magic word and open the wallet to show the bill now under the X.

Right Try out your magic wallet on a classmate.

You will need:
- **two pieces of cardboard 3 in. × 5 in.**
- **four pieces of tape 5 in. long**
- **glue**

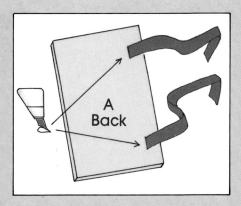

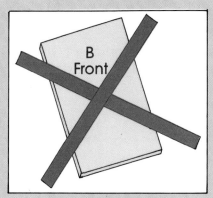

1 Mark the cards A and B on one side (the back). Glue two tapes to the back of card A, about ½ in. in from the ends. Leave to dry.

2 Make an X with the other two tapes on the front of card B so they lie 1 in. in from the ends at the edge (marking this on the card in pencil helps). Do not stick these on.

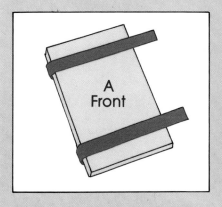

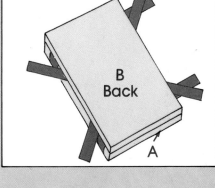

3 Turn over card A so the tapes fall parallel across the front.

4 Carefully lay card B on top of card A so the tapes are all on the inside, still in the positions described in (2) and (3).

5 Glue both the parallel tapes and two ends of the X tapes to the back of card B so that one pair are on each edge, as shown.

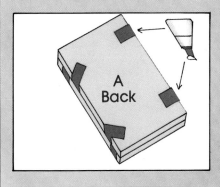

6 Turn the cards over carefully, holding them together, and stick the last two tape ends to the back of card A.

7 For a neat finish cover the outside surfaces of your wallet with sticky paper.

METAL RUBBINGS

On days when the weather is good enough for you to go outside, make a study of some of the many pieces of metalwork that add pattern and interest to streets and public buildings. You can make exact copies of the things you find using the simple and effective method of rubbing over paper.

Try to make a simple rubbing by placing a coin under a piece of paper and shading over it with a soft pencil. Note how the design springs out at you and how clear the detail is.

In the street look for:
- foundation plaques set into walls
- road signs and old milestones and boundary markers in cast iron
- manhole covers, which come in a huge variety of patterns, as do other covers that may be set in the sidewalk in front of many old houses
- the decorative insignia on such items as mailboxes and fire hydrants
- car badges or old-style motoring association badges.

A special brass rubbing center.

MAKING A RUBBING

You will need:
- **a roll of lining paper (not too heavy)**
- **masking tape**
- **crayons**

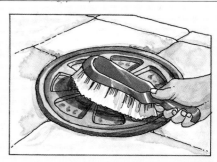

1 Brush or dust the piece you have chosen and make sure it is free of dirt.

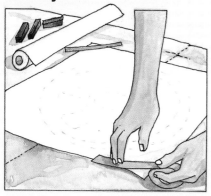

2 Unroll the paper over the piece and fix the paper in place with masking tape.

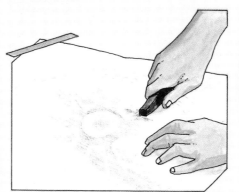

3 Feel over the metalwork gently with your fingers to mark its outline on the paper. Then rub the paper carefully and evenly with the crayon, used lengthwise.

4 Unstick the tape and label the rubbing. Then you could pin it on your wall as decoration.

CHURCH RUBBINGS

In old churches, from the mid-thirteenth century to the mid-seventeenth century, brass slabs were often engraved as memorials and set into the floor or walls. They usually showed a figure, but sometimes just a cross or a religious scene. Occasionally they showed a symbol of the dead person's occupation — for instance, scissors for a tailor. A knight might have his feet resting on a lion (symbolizing courage), while a wool merchant might rest his feet on a sheep. Whole families may be shown on these brasses. But only people who could afford to pay for the brasses and could give money to the church are remembered in this way.

Right An example of a brass rubbing.

COIN-RUBBING PICTURE

Make a coin-rubbing picture using coins of different sizes and foreign coins.

You will need:
- **an assortment of coins**
- **thin plain white paper**
- **thin white cardboard**
- **colored paper**
- **a black crayon**
- **scissors and glue**
- **a clip frame**

1 Place the white paper over a coin. Rub the crayon back and forth over the coin until the markings are clear. Rub several coins in this way.

2 Glue the paper to the thin white card. Smooth out all the air bubbles and leave to dry.

3 Cut the colored paper to the size of your frame and cut out the coins.

4 Make a pattern with the cut-out coins and glue them to the colored paper. Then place your picture in the clip frame.

May Day has a long history and an enormous variety of customs attached to it. The Romans and ancient Celts celebrated the fruitfulness of the earth, with the coming of summer and the sun's warmth. Both decorated and danced around young trees, which were symbols of growth.

In medieval times the custom of going "a-Maying" was widespread. Young people especially would gather flowers and greenery from the woods before dawn. A tree chosen to be the maypole was stripped of all but the top branch (to show new growth), painted in stripes, and decorated with garlands and ribbons before being set up in a central place. A May Queen would be crowned with flowers. The merrymaking continued all day, with colorful parades, feasting, dancing and archery contests.

Scarlet leggings, sashes, ribbons and bells are all a part of the traditional costume for morris dancing.

Sadly, these old customs have gradually disappeared, although some, such as morris dancing, have been revived. Others, such as maypole ribbon dancing, seem only to have been reintroduced early this century.

KEEP SOME MAY CUSTOMS ALIVE

The Celtic May celebration was called Beltane. At Beltane the ancient Celts lit bonfires. All hearth fires would be put out and relit from the central bonfire. People would also leap over the bonfire for good luck. Make a torn-paper collage of a Beltane bonfire. Or make yourself or a friend into the Green Man, who symbolized spring and took part in May Day events in many places in Europe.

BONFIRE COLLAGE

You will need:
- strips of colored tissue
- strips of silver foil
- white tissues
- newspapers and magazines
- glue and a large piece of dark cardboard

1 Create a bonfire by gluing down the colored tissues and silver foil onto the card.

2 Make some Druids out of white tissue and newspaper. Use faces cut from magazines. Add anything else you like.

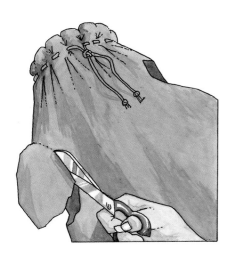

THE GREEN MAN

You will need:
- a large piece of green cloth made into a tube
- a needle and thread or glue
- leaves and twigs
- leafy fabric

1 Pull the tube together at the neck with a drawstring. Cut armholes.

2 Stick or sew on leaves or leaflike material.

3 Put leaves and twigs in your hair.

4 If the tube is wide enough, fix, inside and halfway down, a plastic hoop to make it sway around as you move.

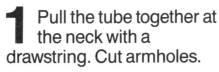

WESAK

Wesak is a Buddhist festival that falls on the day of the full moon in the month of Visakha (May or June); it is also called Visakha Puja. At Wesak, Buddhists in Thailand, Sri Lanka and Burma celebrate three events in the life of the Buddha — his birth, enlightenment and death.

Siddhartha Gautama was a prince who lived around 2,500 years ago and became a monk. Disturbed by seeing old age, sickness and death, he tried to find an answer to why people suffer and whether there is any escape. He found it at last through meditation, that is, thinking deeply. One day, as he watched the morning star rise, he found the wisdom he was searching for. Because he had "seen the light" he became known as the Buddha, "the enlightened one."

The Buddha traveled around India teaching that people should lead kind, unselfish and helpful lives. Followers of his teachings, Buddhists, also meditate in order to achieve a calmness of mind and to see themselves and the world clearly.

When he died at the age of 80, the Buddha passed into a state of complete peace. Every Buddhist aims for this in his or her life.

At Wesak, Buddhists give as generously as they can to the monks and set free caged birds or animals to symbolize the Buddha's feeling for every living creature. They clean their homes and decorate them with flowers, which will also be taken to the temple as an offering. Lanterns are lit at home, and incense and candles are burned at the temple, where a candle-lit parade often ends the day's celebration.

Wesak offerings at a Buddhist temple in Thailand.

WESAK LANTERN

Make this unusual Wesak lantern and stand it in a shallow tray where it will not be knocked over. Several lanterns together look very effective. You will find that the lantern gives off a sweet smell.

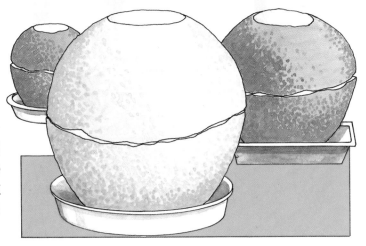

You will need:
- a thick-skinned orange or grapefruit
- a small candle
- a knife
- a spoon
- matches

1 Cut the fruit into halves, horizontally. Cut the inside away from the skin around the edges and clean out with a spoon. Use a sharp knife to cut with and take care!

2 Put a small candle into the base half of the fruit.

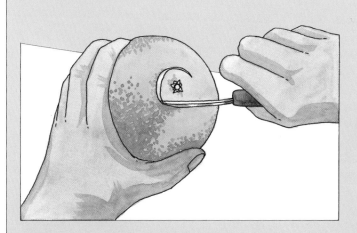

3 Cut a circle 1 in. wide from the center of the top half of the fruit.

4 Ask an adult to light the small candle and put the top on.

Safety note: Be very careful when lighting the lantern. Ask an adult to help you.

NEW GROWTH IN SPRING

The new growth we see every spring does not happen by chance. For every seedling there was a seed just waiting for the right conditions to germinate (put out shoots). Most seeds require water, oxygen and the right temperature; others may have more unusual needs. The seeds of some berried plants are spurred into action by extreme cold or heat.

In the same way, every leaf and flower that appears on trees and shrubs begins as a bud waiting for the same improvement in conditions to swell and open up.

The horse chestnut (buckeye) bud is a good example to study because of its size. It is coated with a sticky resin, which gives it its popular name of "sticky bud." Underneath are several layers of scales which, together with the resin, protect the heart of the bud from damage by rain or insects. Inside, a furry lining protects the tiny flower and leaf shoots from cold and wind until they are strong enough to burst out of the bud (see picture below). By late spring the scales and lining will have been discarded and the tree will be covered with great spikes of pink or white flowers ready for pollination.

GROW A SYCAMORE SEEDLING

Sycamore trees produce a great number of seeds that are spread very efficiently by their "helicopter" wings. They need very little encouragement and will sprout just about anywhere. Because of this, and their fast rate of growth, sycamores are often considered to be weeds.

To see how the seeds germinate, press a few of them down on a shallow layer of soil and keep damp. Sycamores are so ready to sprout that this will usually be enough to start them off.

To grow sycamore trees, follow the instructions opposite.

You will need:

- sycamore seeds
- flowerpot and saucer
- soil or potting compost

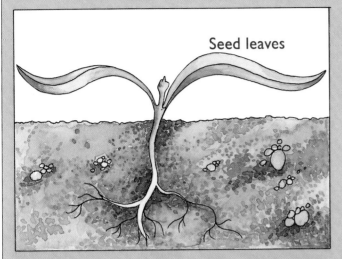

Seed leaves

1 Plant some sycamore seeds in a pot of soil and water regularly. Soon they will split open and send out a root, followed by a shoot with a pair of seed leaves around a tiny bud.

2 Leave to grow. By the summer the seedling should have its first pair of real leaves — the seed leaves wither and drop off.

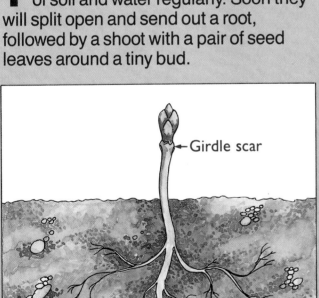

← Girdle scar

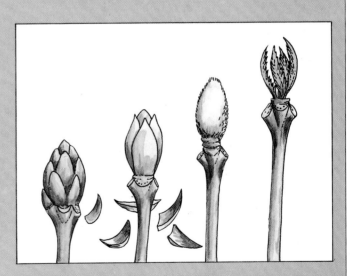

3 In the autumn all the leaves will fall, leaving only a terminal bud and a girdle scar around the stem where the top leaves were.

4 The following spring shoots will grow from the terminal bud and from side buds, the terminal bud "leading the way up." All the time the root system is developing as well.

WILDLIFE GARDEN

You can do a great deal to help the wildlife in your school grounds, garden or area around your home.

BIRDS Put up birdhouses. In spring, hang up bunches of nesting materials — scraps of cloth, wool and so on. Let some leaves and fallen fruits lie on the ground; they will attract insects, which, in turn, will attract birds.

MAMMALS Offer raccoons shelter by packing straw in a woodpile or behind wood left leaning against a wall. Leave some of the undergrowth where slugs and insects live because raccoons like to eat them.

BUTTERFLIES AND MOTHS Butterflies are attracted mostly to bright colors and strong scents. You may like to try to grow some of the flowering plants they prefer in the garden or in window boxes. Just a few of them are buddleia, lavender, sweet william, wallflowers, cornflowers, heather and michaelmas daisies.

Moths generally prefer pale-colored flowers that give off their perfume at dusk and later in the evening, when moths are active. Evening primrose and night-scented stock will attract them.

A small tortoiseshell butterfly on a buddleia, often known as the butterfly bush.

GARDEN POND

Water is very important for all kinds of wildlife. If you have the space, you could try making a garden pond. Stock it with a few aquatic plants and water creatures, such as fish and water snails.

You will need:
- **a pre-formed fiberglass pond** or **plastic sheeting and old carpet**
- **large stones or rocks**
- **fine soil**
- **aquatic (water) plants**

Left Children collecting pond life to put into their school pond.

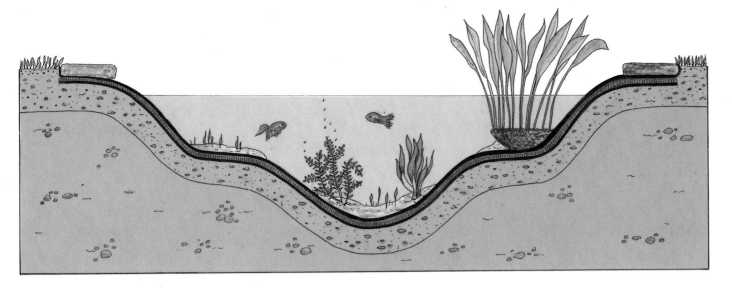

1 Dig a hole and put in whatever you have chosen for the base of the pond. If you are using plastic sheeting, line the hole with carpet first to protect the plastic.

2 Cover the base with a layer of fine soil and plant with aquatic plants before filling with water.

3 Leave to settle for a week or two before you put in any pond animals. You will probably find some have moved in naturally. In spring you could put in a batch of tadpoles.

BIRDBATH

If you do not have a big enough yard or a suitable area at your school for a pond, try making a simple birdbath. One way is to sink an upturned trash can lid in the ground and fill it with water. Another way is shown below.

You will need:
- **plastic sheeting (plastic garbage bag)**
- **8 bricks**

1 Form the bricks into a square, leaving a central space.

2 Spread the sheet over the bricks, tucking it over and under.

3 Fill the bath with water.

Glossary

Aquatic Growing or living in water.

Druid A member of an ancient order of priests.

Effigy A model of a person.

Fasting Going without all or some kinds of food for religious or personal reasons.

Insignia A badge.

Legend A popular story handed down from earlier times which may or may not be true.

Lent A period lasting 40 days (excluding Sundays) before Easter. It is marked by the Christian Church in memory of the 40 days Jesus Christ spent in the wilderness. It is usual to observe some kind of fasting in this period.

Muslims Followers of the Prophet Muhammad.

Oxygen A gas present in the air which is vital for life.

Patron Saint The guardian saint of a person or country.

Pharaoh A ruler of ancient Egypt.

Pollination Causing plants to produce seeds by adding pollen.

Predatory bird A bird that hunts, kills and eats small creatures.

Prey An animal or bird that is attacked and eaten.

Symbol An object that stands for something else (for example, the dove is a symbol of peace).

Temperature The degree of heat or cold.

Terminal bud The bud forming at the end of a stem.

Tracks Footprints or other signs showing that animals or birds have been present.

Tradition A way of doing things, passed down by people over the centuries.

Index

Picture acknowledgments

Cephas Picture Library 4; Chapel Studios 18 (both), cover (top left); Hutchison Library 10; MacQuitty International Collection 24; Oxford Scientific Films 12 (both); Simon Warner 22, 28 (bottom); A. Wharton 26, 28 (top); ZEFA cover (bottom), 6, 14, 16, 21.